# THE
# BACKSTREET BOYS

# THE
# BACKSTREET BOYS

by K. S. Rodriguez

HarperActive™
*A Division of* HarperCollins*Publishers*

*For Christine Squires,*
*remember the days when we were fans?*
*And Ronnie Rodriguez, my Barrow Street Boy*

HarperActive™ is a trademark of HarperCollins Publishers Inc.

ISBN: 0-06-107075-0
Printed in the United States of America
First Edition, 1997

# Contents

## PART ONE: THE BEGINNING

## PART TWO: THE BOYS

## PART THREE: THE BEAT GOES ON

## PART FOUR: BSB FAST FACTS
## AND FUN STUFF

# Acknowledgments

The author gratefully acknowledges Hope Innelli, Lara Comstock, Catherine Daly, and everyone at HarperCollins; Dalita Keumurian, music biz insider, for trying; and my family for their support and patience while I scrambled to get this done: John and Catherine Squires, Arthur Termott, and John and Mary Lou Squires.

PART ONE:

**THE BEGINNING**

**1. They've Got It Goin' On**

**T**eenage girls mob them wherever they go. At concerts, their fans collapse in the aisles. Admirers swarm hotels, radio stations, and record stores just to get a glimpse of their heroes.

No, they're not the Beatles. They're not the New Kids on the Block. They're not Take That.

They're the Backstreet Boys, the R&B pop band with a style all their own.

Their distinctive vocal harmonies, sizzling stage presence, and boyish good looks have skyrocketed these five former unknowns to international superstardom.

The Backstreet Boys have won fans all over the world. Their hits, including "We've Got It Goin' On," "Quit Playin' Games," "Get Down," and "I'll Never Break Your Heart," top international charts. Their self-titled album has gone gold in 11 countries, and platinum in 15. They have sold 10 million albums in 30 countries.

They've received numerous awards, including the 1996 European MTV Viewers' Choice Award. And now that they've conquered audiences overseas, they're ready to come back home to the U.S.

Their long-awaited U.S. debut album, *Backstreet Boys*, hit the stores in the summer of 1997. It blends hip-hop, soul, and passionate ballads and includes all of their European hits, as well as some new songs.

In this book you'll get to know the men behind the music: smart, serious, mature Kevin Richardson, 25; happy-go-lucky party boy A.J. McLean, 19; Brian Littrell, 22, the joker with the charming Southern accent; Nick Carter, at 17 the youngest Backstreet Boy and the biggest international heartthrob; and Howie Dorough, 24, whose loves include dancing and romancing.

Want to know how they got their start? What the boys are like, both onstage and off? What they look for in a girl? Turn the page, and discover everything you've always wanted to know about the Backstreet Boys—and more!

## 2. Getting It Together

It all began in 1993 in Orlando, Florida, the town best known for Disney World. Teen actors A.J. McLean, Howie Dorough, and Nick Carter kept seeing each other at auditions for commercials and TV shows.

"It was kinda funny meeting the same people," Howie remembers. "Especially A.J., who I kept bumping into a lot. He and I would always be there at different agents' offices. I got to know him through a vocal coach we both used. He introduced the two of us."

There can be a lot of downtime at auditions,

and it can get quite boring. So while they waited to be called, the three started hanging out together and quickly became friends. They discovered that they had the same musical tastes, and liked bands such as Boyz II Men and Color Me Badd.

One day, the trio started harmonizing to an old Temptations song. Their voices fit together so well that they decided to form an a cappella group.

Meanwhile in Lexington, Kentucky, Kevin Richardson was dying to get into show business. He heard that there were a lot of opportunities in Orlando since a few movie and television studios had moved down there. He relocated to Florida and took a job at Disney World as a tour guide. In his free time, he sang and wrote music.

A pal of Kevin's heard him singing one day and admired his deep voice. The friend asked if he would be interested in joining a group. He introduced Kevin to Nick, A.J., and Howie.

Kevin was just what the guys were looking for. But they felt something was still missing.

They needed one more member to complete their sound.

Despite auditioning singers from all over Florida, they just couldn't find someone who clicked. That's when Kevin decided to call his cousin Brian Littrell, back in Lexington.

Kevin and Brian grew up together and were always close, sharing a common interest in music and performing in church choir together. Kevin remembered how he and Brian would entertain family members by singing doo-wop and old-time barbershop quartet numbers. He thought Brian would be the perfect fifth member of the group.

Brian was sitting in class when his name was called out over the P.A. system. He was convinced it was bad news—little did he know it was the biggest break of his life!

Brian jumped at the chance to audition for the group and came to Orlando right away. The rest of the group loved his gospel-influenced vocal style. Brian was in.

The only thing left to do was to pick a

name. They took their name from the landmark Backstreet Market, a local teenage hangout in downtown Orlando, and became the Backstreet Boys.

The Boys' voices meshed perfectly without the help of instruments or high-tech recording tricks. They did mostly covers (other bands' songs) at first, but added their own brand of groove, energy, and emotion. The Boys' dance moves made the package complete.

At first, they played at high schools, clubs, at Sea World, and even over the loudspeaker in a pet store! People immediately responded to their sound and the Boys quickly became one of Florida's hottest bands. They started singing original material and released a single, "Tell Me That I'm Dreaming," on an independent label.

They secured a manager, Donna Wright, and started getting bigger gigs at theme parks, state fairs, and music festivals throughout the U.S. The Boys' fan base started to grow and they opened for more famous acts, such as Brandy.

Even though the Boys had cut a single, it wasn't getting much airplay. They desperately wanted a record deal with a larger company. "We'd go to local labels and sing a cappella in their foyers," Howie recalls. "We'd sing anywhere, for anybody."

Their manager knew just what to do. During one of the Backstreet Boys' live appearances, she called a friend at Jive Records. She held up her cellular phone so the record company executive could hear them perform.

Jive Records liked what they heard. And it wasn't just the music that caught their attention. The fervor of the fans signaled to them that the Backstreet Boys were a hot commodity.

The Boys' wish came true, and Jive immediately signed them on. Jive had high hopes for the combo, and the company wouldn't be disappointed.

That day five stars were born. Kevin, Brian, A.J., Nick, and Howie took off on a one-way trip to superstardom. And they haven't looked back since.

## 3. The Express to Success

Judging from the Backstreet Boys' good looks and cool rhythms, Jive Records had a hunch that they just might have the next New Kids on the Block or Take That on their hands. Plus, they recognized the Backstreet Boys' wide range of abilities. They could sing and dance hip-hop on one song, then serenade a crowd with a soulful ballad the next.

With all this potential, the record company didn't want to waste any time. The Boys immediately flew to Cheiron studios in Stockholm, Sweden. With the help of Denniz PoP of Ace of

Base, they recorded "We've Got It Goin' On."

Jive released this danceable tune with the infectious backbeat in Europe in 1995. English audiences were the first to jump on the BSB bandwagon. The single instantly received heavy airplay, and climbed the British charts. When the Boys were invited to perform on the popular television show *Top of the Pops*, it was clear they had a smash hit.

As Brian explains, "Over there they had a bunch of what's called 'boy groups,' so we had a ready-made market. But since we were Americans, we were a fresh new sound for Europe."

The Boys also had more of a stylistic edge than some of the other boy groups. But their main ingredient was talent. Brian says, "We were more than just a bunch of pretty guys. We could sing."

The music industry started to pay attention to the hot new quintet. *Billboard* magazine praised their first effort, saying that "We've Got It Goin' On" would "connect quickly with rhythm/

crossover and top 40 tastemakers. . . . Odds are good that they will go home winners."

On the heels of "We've Got It Goin' On," Jive released the second single, the ballad "I'll Never Break Your Heart." This song was also a smash hit in England.

There was no stopping the Backstreet Boys. They soared to the top of the charts and quickly became the favorites of audiences all over Europe. Soon their popularity spread to Asia. Radio stations from Germany to Singapore were playing the two singles in their heavy rotation.

By the end of 1995, less than one year after the release of their first single, the Backstreet Boys nabbed the Smash Hits Award for the Best New Tour Act and were voted "#1 Boy Band" by viewers of VIVA, a television network in Germany.

And all of this before the Boys even came out with their first album.

In April 1996, the successful singles were followed up by the release of their long-awaited debut album, *Backstreet Boys.* Their third single, "Get Down (You're the One for Me)," was released at the same time.

It seemed the Boys could do no wrong. The album and "Get Down" raced to the top of the charts. By the summer of 1996, fans were clamoring for a concert tour.

The Boys were more than happy to oblige.

Their first major headlining tour was a sell-out. The boys had 57 shows throughout Europe, with stops in countries such as England, Germany, Belgium, and Poland.

Meanwhile the awards kept coming: They were named "Best Newcomers" at Germany's VIVA Comet Awards and at London's Red Nose Awards. The Boys were especially proud of winning the European MTV Viewers' Choice Award in London. They had stiff competition from Oasis and the Spice Girls, but proved even hotter than those two popular bands.

In England, they were invited back to *Top of the Pops,* making five appearances in one year. In Montreal, Canada, "Get Down" unseated their own "We've Got It Goin' On" video as the Video Battle Champion of Musique on Plus television. In fact, *The Backstreet Boys Home Video* went diamond in Canada, which is platinum times ten!

They became the fastest-selling new group in Southeast Asia. The debut album sold over 600,000 copies there in just ten weeks.

That primed the Boys for another sell-out tour, this time of the Asian Pacific Islands, with stops in Australia, Korea, Hong Kong, Japan, Malaysia, and New Zealand.

They released their fourth single, "Quit Playin' Games (With My Heart)," in November 1996. One month later, the Boys embarked on their second European tour, with stops in Austria, France, Norway, and Sweden.

They also toured Canada, performing in Quebec, Ontario, and British Columbia. The Canadian concerts sold out in less than 20 minutes and drew as many as 70,000 screaming fans.

The international frenzy for the Backstreet

Boys had begun. Europe, Asia, and Canada had not seen this kind of phenomenon since Take That. And they may never see anything like it again!

# 4. Fan Frenzy

**S**oon screaming, fainting fans followed the Boys everywhere. In January 1996, 35 girls collapsed when the Boys performed at a shopping mall in Montreal.

In Hamburg, Germany, police were called in to control the hysterical crowd when the BSBs made an appearance at a local radio station in February.

In March, the Boys had to leave a television station in Munich, Germany, when fans surrounded the building and blocked the entrances.

They gained such a following that Nick Carter's father had to build a fence around his entire Florida home after German fans took chunks of the lawn with them as souvenirs.

The Boys were amazed at their following. A.J. had never been much of a ladies' man in high school. He couldn't believe girls were literally crying over him at concerts!

Brian says in awe, "We've done signings in record stores where there've been over three thousand people. One time in Germany there was a riot. The girls busted through the barriers and we had to leave. But we know it's only because our fans want to get closer to us, and we really do love them."

Any BSB concert guarantees a commotion. Fans shriek when the guys unbutton their shirts and show off their buff bodies. They nearly faint when each Boy pulls a girl from the audience to dance with them onstage. They swoon when Kevin presents a blushing girl with a rose, and they scream when Nick pounds out a hot rhythm on his drums.

Once, Howie mentioned in an interview that he liked Gummi Bears. As soon as that magazine hit the stands, fans started bringing the candies to concerts and tossing them onstage. Some female fans have thrown underwear onstage, too!

The fans will do anything to get close to these hunks. They've even been found hiding in the luggage compartment of the BSB tour bus. Now security guards check every nook and cranny thoroughly before the Boys move on to their next gig.

Do the Boys tire of the frenzy they've created? Never. "I think it's cool, real cool," says A.J. Howie agrees. "It's very flattering."

Brian even regrets not being able to spend as much time with BSB fans as he used to. "As we've gotten more well known, more people want to meet us and I worry that the ones who were there at the beginning feel neglected," he says.

While superstardom does have its downside, it also has its perks. The Boys have been able to meet some of their idols during their travels, including Color Me Badd, Boyz II Men, Whitney Houston, and Bobby Brown.

The Boys were especially honored to meet an early influence: the Temptations. The days of killing time while waiting for auditions came flooding back to A.J., Howie, and Nick when the Boys sang for their idols backstage once.

The Temptations took the Boys under their wing and even offered some words of wisdom. Howie told *BB* magazine, "One of the guys said 'In this business, you are in show business,' and he emphasized that you have to know the business part as well as the entertaining part."

The Boys are no dummies, so they took the Temptations' advice and set up their own corporation: The Backstreet Boys Inc. They are shareholders in their own company, making decisions together as a group about their finances.

The Temptations weren't the only band to give the Backstreet Boys good advice. Robbie

Williams of Take That told the Boys to never lose sight of who they are and what they have.

It doesn't look like fame will go to their heads. Down-to-earth Brian appreciates the people who made him a superstar. "I want everyone to realize that the fans always have been, and always will be, the most important thing," he says. "After all, we'd be nothing without them."

# 5. The Big Homecoming

With their huge success overseas, the Boys are anxious to see what will happen at home in the U.S. Kevin says, "We want our teachers, friends, and family to see what we've done with our lives."

The Boys also admit to missing their home country's food. A.J. told *Bop* magazine that "whenever I'm in different cultures, I always make a point of trying the local foods. But nothing ever beats good American cooking."

Howie adds, "We are definitely ready for success at home." Judging from their track record, it won't be hard for this fantastic five to sweep the American audiences onto the Backstreet bandwagon.

The *Backstreet Boys* album is being released in the U.S. in the summer of 1997. Their American debut features all the hits from their European album, including "We've Got It Goin' On," "Anywhere for You," and "Quit Playin' Games (With My Heart)," which is the first single.

The album also features new tracks, too, such as a cover of PM Dawn's "Set Adrift on Memory Bliss," which has new lyrics written especially for the Backstreet Boys, and "All I Have to Give," produced by Full Force.

Before the album's release, the Boys are returning home to Orlando to remix, record some new songs, and shoot new videos. To promote the long-awaited debut, they'll spend time in Los Angeles, New York, Hawaii, and Texas. They'll even kick off a mini U.S. tour, appearing at Wal-Mart stores across the country.

The American media has flocked to cover

the international superstars even before their album was released in the U.S. They've been featured in *Billboard* magazine, *USA Today*, and the *New York Daily News*. They have graced the covers of *Bop, Teen Beat, 16, Tutti Frutti, Tiger Beat,* and *SuperTeen.*

The Boys are glad to be back, and the American audience is proving to be hungry for this supergroup. According to Nick, "We've always wanted to bring it back home. But we wanted to make sure we brought it back strong."

PART TWO:

THE BOYS

## 6. Cool, Calm, Collected Kevin Richardson

**M**eet Kevin. At 25, he's the oldest Backstreet Boy. Tall, dark, and gorgeous, with sparkling green eyes, Kevin has an onstage personality that is absolutely magnetic. But what was his life like prior to stardom?

Kevin Scott Richardson was born in Lexington, Kentucky, on October 3, 1972. This Backstreet Boy is originally a back*woods* boy: He lived on a farm until he was nine, then moved to a log cabin!

"I had a great childhood," Kevin recalls. "I loved school, played Little League football, rode horses and dirt bikes, and sang into a hairbrush in front of my bedroom mirror."

Kevin grew up performing in the church choir and in chorus at school and got his first keyboard when he was a freshman in high school. His first gigs were talent shows and weddings.

Now, Kevin and his keyboard are inseparable. He jokes that he even takes up four airplane seats traveling with it.

When Kevin was in his late teens, he moved down to Orlando, looking to get into the entertainment business. First he worked as a tour guide at Disney World, and later he played Aladdin.

Levelheaded Kevin is a Libra, which means he strives for balance and harmony. Libras like Kevin are happiest when things are peaceful and orderly.

Libra men are intellectual, athletic, and talkative, though Kevin admits to being occasionally bashful. "Sometimes when I'm with a girl I can be really shy because I'm afraid I'll say something wrong," he says.

Kevin displays the trademark Libra sense of humor, keen intuition, and careful diplomacy. Balanced Libras rarely like to create a stir, but Kevin just can't help it—after all, he *is* a BSB. In addition, he's serious and sensitive. "It's my nature," Kevin says. "I've always been that way."

He's a natural leader and a perfectionist. His bandmate pals gave him the nickname "Train" because, being the oldest, he likes to take control of the other guys.

Charm is the Libra's secret weapon in courtship, and Kevin has a truckload of it.

He loves girls who like to dress up, but who also feel comfortable in a big sweater or one of his shirts. But the most important thing to Kevin is having someone he can really talk to. "She's got to be intelligent and confident about what she's saying." Kevin also likes clever women who have good manners.

He told a French-Canadian magazine that "I want someone real, someone whose internal values match what's outside. . . . When I see her

I'll know her right away, that she's the one I was waiting for."

He's currently single, but enjoys dating. "When I'm going out with a girl, I like to be with her all the time, and it's important we talk about everything."

But Kevin finds it hard to have a relationship when he's busy recording and touring. "Right now, everything in my world is revolving around the Backstreet Boys."

Though he wouldn't rule out a long-distance relationship, Kevin believes that "seeing someone for only a few hours a month isn't synonymous with romance."

When things calm down for this hunky superstar, he says he would like to catch up with old friends and put time into a serious relationship.

Kevin is clearly a family man. On the liner notes of the European release of *Backstreet Boys,* he thanks his brothers and his mother, calling her the "most wonderful woman I know."

Tragically, Kevin lost his father to cancer when he was just a teenager. He wrote, "He was the greatest man I'll ever know. If I can be half the man you were as a father, a husband, and as a friend, then I will consider myself to be successful. I miss you, Dad." Kevin dedicated the album to his father's memory.

Kevin's attachment to his family makes him dream about having his own one day. "I want a family," he told *Bop* magazine. "I love kids. I can't wait to have a family."

When asked to describe himself, Kevin says he is "an honest person. I don't play games, I say what's on my mind, and treat people with respect."

He's sensitive and isn't afraid to show his feelings. He told *TV Hits* magazine, "I cry in movie theaters all the time. I get that from my grandfather—we're a real sentimental family. Brian's like that as well. When we got our first gold record, we bawled like babies!"

What does this cutie do for kicks? He enjoys sports and keeping his bod in shape.

Some of his favorite activities are waterskiing, weightlifting, swimming, surfing, basketball, and hockey.

In more relaxed moments he enjoys writing songs on his keyboard, strumming a bass, or cozying up with his pet cat, Quincy. When he has time, he kicks back and watches TV, preferably comedies like *Roseanne*. Kevin also loves to dance, onstage and off. He's even a qualified ballroom dance instructor!

Kevin loves Asian food. His favorite colors are royal blue, purple, and black. CDs by R. Kelly, Prince, Babyface, and Teddy Riley can be found in his collection.

What does this handsome hottie think about life on the road? "A lot of fun, a lot of work, and sometimes a little lonely. But it's what I've always dreamed of!"

# 7. Heartthrob Howie Dorough: Mr. Romance

**H**oward Dwaine Dorough, better known as Howie D, was born August 22, 1973, in Orlando, Florida. He is the baby of the family—the youngest of six children—and a natural-born performer. At the age of three, he would jump onto his grandmother's bed and burst into song.

Howie has a million-dollar smile that drives fans wild. He's easygoing, outgoing, and suave. Half Irish and half Puerto Rican, Howie has the looks of a Latin lover and he can speak the languages of Spanish, and *love*, fluently.

As a child, Howie D sang in choir, took dancing lessons, and performed in community theater and commercials.

As he grew older, he won roles in a Nickelodeon pilot called *Welcome Freshmen* and the films *Parenthood,* which starred comedian Steve Martin, and *Cop and a Half,* with Burt Reynolds.

Not surprisingly, Howie's star sign is Leo, right on the cusp of Virgo. Leos like to be the center of attention, and Howie, with his soulful falsetto, is always in the limelight.

Leos like Howie are natural extroverts who love to laugh. Their generous and loyal nature makes Leos great friends to have! Virgos are also known to be incredibly faithful as a friend and lover.

Both Leos and Virgos are typically very neat, and Howie has been known to iron everything—even his pajamas! Like a Virgo, he is meticulous about his appearance and always looks hotter than a roaring bonfire.

Leos have their share (sometimes more) of

bad luck. In fact, Howie D is the Backstreet Boy whose luggage has been lost most often! His hip-hop clothes and boxers have frequently ended up on the opposite side of the world. But he takes life's ups and downs with his usual good humor.

Howie has a generous nature and devotes time to charities and good causes. In high school, he was involved in a peer counseling group. He would reach out to other kids and talk to them about living "a clean life, having fun, going to school, avoiding drugs." He and his bandmates are now involved in the Ronald McDonald charity and SADD, Students Against Destructive Decisions.

The other BSBs recognize Howie's big heart and gave him the nickname "Sweet D." He often acts as the peacemaker whenever the Boys have disagreements.

Leos are known to create romantic fire-works, and Howie is no exception. He admits to being a hard-core romantic who loves to wine, dine, and enjoy sentimental moments with his dates.

His ideal girlfriend is "someone who is always looking at things in a positive way, not in a negative way, and who knows what she wants in life and how to go about getting it."

Though most Virgos are bachelors, Howie claims he would like to get married someday, when he finds the girl of his dreams. He envisions his wife to be a "loving, faithful, honest girl with character and a good heart."

And while Howie wouldn't mind a date with Cindy Crawford, he prefers "more natural-looking girls." A great sense of humor, plenty of self-confidence, and sparkling blue eyes wouldn't hurt, either. But there's one thing he can't stand: girls who are arrogant.

He prefers a spontaneous girl who will do anything on the spur of the moment. He says his dream girl wouldn't mind dancing to a slow song in a restaurant—even if no one else was dancing.

Howie's girl has to be full of hugs, too. He loves affection and thinks it's nice when fans give him gifts like teddy bears.

It's also important to Sweet D that his

sweetheart be supportive of his career, and be "someone I can bring home to my mom." It's a must to Howie that his family and friends accept his girlfriend.

What does Howie consider a dream date? He says he likes "to surprise a girl, like take her out for a weekend" somewhere on a beach or "take her out for dinner, then go to the movies, go out dancing, then probably walk out on the beach at night."

What if he were in colder weather? Howie says he'd cuddle up with his honey out on a terrace "under fur jackets and a blanket" watching the snow fall.

Though he dreams of a whirlwind romance and a long-term commitment, Howie is single. The rumors that Howie is going out with one of the Spice Girls are completely false. Like the other BSBs, he is so busy that he finds it hard to make time for a serious relationship right now.

In his spare moments, Howie likes to work out, water-ski, dance, watch movies, and play racquetball. Like Kevin, he says his favorite cuisine is Asian, and his favorite music includes that of Jon Secada and Bobby Brown.

To relax, Howie likes to play guitar, which he's just learned. Having spent years concentrating on his singing, Howie regrets he never had time for the instrument before. He also likes to chill out watching sitcoms like *Seinfeld* and *Married . . . With Children*.

In a nutshell, Howie D is a sweet and tender romantic. And what fan wouldn't jump at the chance to spend a quiet evening alone with him?

Howie appreciates all his fans for their support. "I see at every show some girls in the audience I could fall in love with," he has said. He thanks them in a characteristically charming statement in the liner notes of the album:

"And last but not least I'd like to give my deepest thanks, from the bottom of my heart, to all the Backstreet Boys fans out there; we could not do this without you! Keep the Backstreet Pride Alive."

# 8. The Joker's Wild: Brian Littrell

**D**id someone say Southern gentleman? That's Brian Thomas Littrell, the only Backstreet Boy with an adorable drawl. Brian was born on February 20, 1975, in Lexington, Kentucky.

Brian spent a good part of his youth singing at local churches and revivals. Away from church, however, his ear was glued to Top 40 stations, listening to artists such as Hammer, Boyz II Men, and Bobby Brown.

Brian is cheerful and energetic. When he is onstage, he looks as if he is truly having the time of his life.

His trademark is his great sense of humor. He loves to laugh, make people laugh, and flash his heart-stopping smile.

"I've laughed so much," he told *Alive and Kicking* magazine, "that my stomach hurt. . . . When you are around a lot of people who are laughing and everyone laughs and the whole world joins in and no one can stop . . . it hurts!"

Mostly, Brian likes to make others laugh by making faces, telling jokes, or pulling pranks. He counts funnyman Jim Carrey as one of his idols.

"I guess I'm just a happy kind of guy," he told *TV Hits* magazine. "I don't see any point in being miserable. Probably the only time you'll see me low is when I'm sick."

Brian's looks are not as smolderingly sexy as those of the other Backstreet Boys; rather, his appeal is in his clean-cut, all-American wholesomeness. Fans go crazy over Brian's baby blues.

He was born on the cusp of Aquarius and

Pisces, and it's obvious that he has the best of both of these highly creative, fiercely independent signs.

Like a typical Aquarius, Brian enjoys good times with his many good friends. One of his closest buddies is his bandmate Nick. They've been known to call each other "Frick" and "Frack."

"Nick is like the kid brother I never had," Brian says. The two hit it off as soon as they met. Brian was impressed with Nick's energy and his tremendous vocal power.

Nick and Brian hang out together constantly. They enjoy playing video games and tossing a football around, even though Brian says Nick beats him all the time.

Brian is traditional and old-fashioned, and would one day like to settle down. He will probably shun commitment for a while, though, until he meets the girl of his dreams. When he finds that girl, Brian swears he will make her Mrs. Littrell, despite having mentioned more than once his affection for Sandra

Bullock and Pamela Anderson Lee.

What does Brian look for in a girl? He likes long hair, but he feels personality is more important. Brian also admits, "Eyes are very appealing to me," and he'd like to end up with "someone who can treat me like a normal person."

Even though Brian is known to joke around, he takes love "very seriously," and adds, "I can't see myself without a girl who's intelligent, a girl who shares my values, religiously or morally, and my interests. She'd have to have a good sense of humor . . . determination and lots of energy."

What's Brian's dream date? "A flawless evening over a candlelit dinner." Or a night at home, where he would make dinner and "cuddle up and watch a movie," preferably a romantic one like *Sleepless in Seattle* or *While You Were Sleeping*.

According to Brian's astrology, he makes an excellent companion who enjoys the best of everything, and likes doing things on a whim.

Brian is the spontaneous type who would plan a lot of surprises for his girl. Once he even put a dozen roses in a girlfriend's locker to surprise her at school.

Like all the Boys, Brian deeply appreciates his fans and the efforts they make. Brian's favorite gift from a fan was a tie. A tie might sound like a boring present, but this fan drew all of the musical notes and lyrics to "I'll Never Break Your Heart" on it. Another of his favorite fan gifts was a basketball hoop. When asked if he would date a fan, Brian responded with a resounding "Yes!"

Because of his dual star signs, Brian has many good love matches, including Aries, Taurus, Cancer, Scorpio, and Capricorn girls.

In his spare time, Brian enjoys weight-lifting, listening to music such as Boyz II Men or Bobby Brown, watching *The Fresh Prince of Bel-Air*, or playing with his cat, Missy. He also likes to play basketball, which is how he got his nickname, "B-Rok."

He has down-home tastes when it comes

to food. His favorite meal is macaroni and cheese. His favorite color? Forest green.

Though he's always joking, Brian considers himself a sensitive guy. He's not ashamed to admit that he is afraid of heights and that he bites his fingernails.

It seems many fans wouldn't mind putting up with those tiny flaws just to get close to their favorite Backstreet Boy, Brian "B-Rok" Littrell.

## 9. Get Down and Party With A.J. McLean

"**P**aaaarty!" That's one of A.J.'s favorite words. This fun-loving Backstreet Boy is always ready to have a good time.

Alexander James McLean was born on January 9, 1978, in West Palm Beach, Florida. Like the other BSBs, A.J. took to performing at an early age, starring as Dopey in *Snow White and the Seven Dwarfs* in grade school. He enjoyed it so much that he went on to roles in musicals such as *The King and I* and *Fiddler on the Roof.*

By the time A.J. was in junior high, he had

already snagged a part in Nickelodeon's *Hi Honey, I'm Home* and went on to appear in many Nickelodeon and Disney Channel shows. While doing all of this, and attending school, A.J. also found the time to take dance and acting lessons.

A.J. is a Capricorn, a star sign that is known for persistence and dedication. Capricorns are goal-setters and goal-achievers and they climb to the top of whatever field they are in. That describes A.J. to a T!

Capricorns enjoy life, and A.J. is no exception. On his last birthday, the Boys were in New York City. They decided to throw A.J. a party at Hackers, Hitters, and Hoops, an interactive sports and recreation center.

A.J. brought his number one lady as his date: his mom, Denise. A.J. and his mom are very close, and she takes an avid interest in the Backstreet Boys. She's in charge of their scheduling and has even started fan clubs for the Boys abroad.

At the party, A.J. and the rest of the Boys had a blast, hitting baseballs in batting cages, playing video games, driving a few golf balls on a simulated course, and challenging each other to games of Ping-Pong. Of course, great tunes blasted over the sound system all night long and A.J. was presented with a delicious birthday cake.

Although A.J. had a great time celebrating his 19th birthday, he says it was his 18th that was most memorable to date.

That year, the Boys' managers threw A.J. and Nick a joint birthday party. Over 200 guests came to help blow out the candles.

Things got a little out of hand, but that was just fine with A.J. "The guys threw me in the pool and I rubbed cake down Nick's shirt and in his hair," he reports. The crazy guy stayed up until six in the morning, dancing and chatting the night away.

But this party boy is no stranger to late nights. A.J. enjoys dancing to '70s tunes or hip-hop all night long in clubs around the world. His dream party would be in a cool club and the guest list would include Jim Carrey, the Spice Girls, and Geena Davis.

A.J.'s idea of fun is "being able to do what you want and not care about the consequences. Doing things that you never thought you'd do. Like skydiving naked!"

He's definitely the most flamboyant member of the BSBs. He sports flashy jewelry and is a nonstop talker. The other guys say he's constantly on the phone, or telling someone a story.

So is this fast talker smooth with the girls? Surprisingly, he says no. "The few times I've been with someone," he told *Le Lundi* magazine, "things went very wrong." Tragically, his first crush was killed in a car accident. "It was a shock to me. It took me a long time to get over that and love someone again."

Then, when he was 15, his girlfriend moved to California without letting him know! The last time he was in love, he wrote a love poem for his honey, only to find her kissing another guy.

It hasn't been easy for A.J., but he still believes in love. He's certain that fate will bring him the girl of his dreams.

And what kind of girl might she be? A.J. likes to be around girls with charisma and self-confidence. "I'd like her to be pretty, of course, but she'd have to be, first and foremost, sensitive and intelligent, have a thirst for learning, and a good sense of humor."

Though A.J. likes to have a lot of laughs, he also would like his mate to have a serious side.

What could a lucky girl expect from a date with A.J.? His dream date would consist of eating McDonald's (an addiction for him!) or pizza and then renting a movie like *Ghost*. "I don't want to show off. I want to be myself," he has said.

He also envisions "sitting in front of a log fire with hot chocolate and marshmallows and some mellow music playing. It'd be great if the moon was shining in, the lights were low, and it was cold outside."

A.J. says he'd date a fan and "if she just swept me off my feet, I probably wouldn't see her as a fan." Outgoing A.J. has been known to invite fans to breakfast, and even call a fan who had given him her number!

"Not long ago, I called some girls in Germany," he confides. "They were totally surprised when I said, 'Hi, this is A.J. from the Backstreet Boys.' We talked about school, hobbies, and I invited [them] to our next concert."

It's clear that A.J. is a well-rounded guy. Off the concert stage, he enjoys puppeteering and ventriloquism. In fact, A.J. worked as a puppeteer on the Nickelodeon show *Welcome Freshmen,* the same show bandmate Howie briefly appeared on.

He also likes to dance, write poetry, play basketball, draw cartoons, play volleyball, and shoot pool. He has a pet dachshund named Toby Wan Kenobi, and he likes to relax listening to music on his headphones or watching television comedies like *Married . . . With Children.*

Friendly A.J. has a lot of buddies, including "a lot of close girl friends," and claims he even has more girl friends than boy friends.

A.J. feels especially close to all of the Backstreet Boys. They've given him the nickname Bone (though they're not saying why). In the *Backstreet Boys* liner notes, A.J. effusively thanks his partners: "To My Boys—B-Rok, Kev, Nick, and Howie—thanks fellas for your patience with me and being there for me anytime I was in need. (Go Backstreet.)"

# 10. Nice Guy Nick Carter

**L**ast but not least is the youngest of the bunch: Nickolas Gene Carter. Nick was born January 28, 1980, in Jamestown, New York. He's the biggeest heartthrob of the BSBs, with his blond hair, blue eyes, and baby face. He says he never tires of being called cute, and loves all the attention he's been getting.

Nick's father owned a music club, so groovin' is in his blood. He started dancing when he was still in diapers!

Nick is the oldest child in the Carter family. He has four younger siblings: two sisters and twin brothers.

Nick's first acting experience was playing the lead in his fourth-grade production of *The Phantom of the Opera*. Shortly after, his family moved to Florida. He also took voice, drum, and guitar lessons. With so many other talents, his wonderful singing voice was almost overlooked!

Soon, young Nick went on to win talent shows and sing at Tampa Bay Buccaneers football games.

He also won roles in television commercials and was even offered a gig with Disney, but he decided to join the Backstreet Boys instead. Thousands of fans all over the world are awfully glad he made that decision!

Nick is an Aquarius, which might explain his strong friendships, particularly with bandmate Brian. Aquarius men are outgoing and like to be surrounded by people. Aquarians like Nick are generous friends and great listeners. They are the kind of companions people tend to confide in. They are the type of guy who would ask a girl a lot of questions and truly be interested in what she had to say.

Though Aquarians like to develop close relationships, they are dreamers who enjoy their independence. Some Aquarians may come off as cool and in control, but they do have a well of emotions bubbling below the surface.

Aquarian men like to be pursued, rather than being the pursuer. Nick is no exception, though he admits, "I haven't been in love yet." He explains that he's still young and still a little shy around girls.

It's hard to believe that a guy as hot as Nick would be shy, but he is easily embarrassed. Once, to tease him, the guys threw him out of his dressing room in nothing but his underwear! To make matters worse, a swarm of girls were waiting outside and saw him in his drawers!

What kind of girl does Nick go for? He prefers long hair, and would like a girl who creates a challenge for him. Most important, he says, is to find someone "with a good heart and a good personality." He likes being around girls who are self-confident and who don't smoke. He adds that he "values the inside qualities more than any beauty."

Nick says he would be a faithful boyfriend who would love spoiling his sweetheart. He looks for girls who are honest, loyal, and romantic. He wouldn't want to be with a girl who would lie or cheat on him. He says he's a "down-to-earth kind of guy and I hope that's all my girl would need."

What is his idea of a dream date? Nick says, "Just to have fun . . . I like to make the most of my time together with a date."

Nick said he, too, would date a fan if he liked her. He tries to answer all of his fan mail personally, but judging from the amount he receives, it must be a difficult task.

Nick is mobbed wherever he goes. "It's surprising," he says, "but really cool." And though Nick can deal with the price of fame, he admits that he's not too happy when fans pull his hair. Recently he got his blond locks cut short to discourage further assaults on his scalp.

What is he like in private? Nick enjoys playing video games, especially with his buddy

B-Rok. He brings his Playstation on tour with him, but has been accused by the other guys of hogging it. He enjoys spending time with his family, and when he's not on the road, he lives with his parents, siblings, his terrier Boo Boo, and his cat Pinky.

His favorite food is pizza, and his favorite color is green. In his free time Nick loves scuba diving, and he is a certified diver. He also enjoys motorboating, fishing, playing football, and reading poetry. Nick watches *The X-Files*, *Mad About You,* and *The Simpsons.* He listens to a variety of music, including AC/DC, Oasis, Kriss Kross, Prince, Jodeci, Lenny Kravitz, Mary J. Blige, Nirvana, and even country music.

Of all the BSBs, he's the closest with Brian. Brian has this to say about "the kid brother [he] never had": "I'm proud of the way he handles everything that comes along and how he's matured. . . . Nick's always real straight-faced and gets the job done the best he can."

Cool Kevin's "Got It Goin' On."
(© 1997 B. Khan/Retna Ltd.)

Here he gives the people what
they want . . . more of him!
(© 1996 Mark Allan/Alpha London/Globe Photos)

B
S
B

Howie flashes a big smile for the cameras.
(© 1996 David Fisher/London Features)

Sometimes the guys get a little carried away!
(© 1997 Mark Cairns/Retna Ltd.)

Brian loves to joke around, but is a good sport, too.

B
S
B

A.J. cracks a "Quit Playin' Games (With My Heart)" kind of smile.
(© 1996 Jeff Spicer/Alpha London/Globe Photos

A true sign of love for his fans—
A.J. gives autographs everywhere he goes.
(© 1996 Jeff Spicer/Alpha London/Globe Photos)

B
S
B

**Put your hands together for Nick—
the youngest Backstreet Boy!**
(© 1995 Nick Tansley/Retna Ltd.)

**Here he is pumped to enjoy
a rare day off.**
(© 1996 C. Vooren/Sunshine/Retna Ltd.)

**The Backstreet Boys sing a capella live at the Hard Rock Cafe in London.**
(©1996 Dave Morgan/Alpha London/Globe Photos)

**It should be against the law to be this hot!**
(© 1996 Mark Allan/Alpha London/Globe Photos)

**Harmonizing is real teamwork!**
(© 1995 Jeff Spicer/Alpha London/Globe Photos)

**The Backstreet Boys are at their best in the spotlight!**
(©1997 Mark Allan/Alpha London/Globe Photos)

B
S
B

You've got to hand it to them—the Backstreet Boys leave their mark wherever they go.

(© 1996 David Fisher/London Features)

In the end, they do it all for the fans.

(© 1996 Ilpo Musto/London Features)

PART THREE:

THE BEAT GOES ON

11. The Songs

**T**he Backstreet Boys' American debut features all their European hits plus brand-new, previously unreleased tracks. New tracks include a remake of PM Dawn's "Set Adrift on Memory Bliss"; "If You Stay," which was originally on the *Booty Call* soundtrack; "Don't Leave Me," a catchy rockin' number; "Tell Me That I'm Dreamin'," the first independent single they released; and "Tender Love," a song in which A.J. shares the contents of a letter he has written. The album has fourteen tracks in all. Here are some of the highlights:

## "WE'VE GOT IT GOIN' ON"

written by Denniz PoP, Max Martin, and Herbert Crichlow

*Everybody groove to the music/Everybody jam . . .*

It's hard not to jam to this lively, funky tune. This was the Boys' first major single, and it's no surprise that it was an instant smash. The chorus is infectious. It makes you want to get up and dance! The Boys had help from Denniz PoP of Ace of Base fame on this one, which they recorded in Sweden.

## "ANYWHERE FOR YOU"

written by Gary Baker and Wayne Perry

*I'd walk halfway around the world/For just one kiss from you . . .*

Picture sitting in front of a roaring fire with your honey, this song playing quietly in the background. Talk about instant romance! Or better yet, imagine slow dancing with your favorite BSB pulling you close. Melodious and moving, this tune is surefire kindling for romance.

### "GET DOWN (YOU'RE THE ONE FOR ME)"

written by Bülent Aris and Toni Cottura

*Get down, Get down/And move it all around . . .*

     This tune is destined to be a club favorite. There's no doubt that the funky backbeat will have crowds swaying together in unison. As an added bonus, A.J. busts a rap with Smooth T. from Fun Factory.

### "I'LL NEVER BREAK YOUR HEART"

written by Eugene Wilde and Albert Manno

*Now all I ask is a chance/To prove that I love you . . .*

     Who wouldn't give dreamy Kevin that chance, with his sexy deep voice pleading for you and his gorgeous green eyes staring into your soul! This sweet love ballad is the perfect prom or wedding song.

### "QUIT PLAYIN' GAMES (WITH MY HEART)"

written by Max Martin and Herbert Crichlow

*Even in my heart I see/You're not bein' true to me . . .*

     Another cool tune, this is the first single from the American debut. It's already climbing the charts, and it can't miss. Brian and Nick share the vocals on this catchy dance-pop song. Everyone can relate to Brian's wish that he could turn back time.

## "JUST TO BE CLOSE TO YOU"
written by Tim Grant and Michael Gray
*It's the only thing I want to do . . .*

This track really shows off the Boys' heavenly harmonies. It's a little bit funky, a little bit sexy, and a whole lot smooth. The boys show off their a cappella style at the very end. When all the instruments fade away, the listener is left with the soaring sound of the Boys' bare voices.

## "BOYS WILL BE BOYS"
written by Jolyon Skinner and Veit Renn
*I've got something so incredible in my eyes . . .*

This dance tune is irresistible, and one of the BSBs' best live numbers. The energy rocks the house when the Boys get down and chant "Go! Go! Go!" It's a great tune that is guaranteed to kick off any party.

## "EVERY TIME I CLOSE MY EYES"

written by Eric Foster White

*When you close your eyes do you think about me? . . .*

This romantic, up-tempo love song is hot—perfect music for a date on the beach. It's smooth, stylin', lovin' fun, and Kevin's rap is a sexy highlight.

## 12. Dream Boys

They're fun, smart, sensitive, exciting, talented, and, above all, gorgeous. These honeys can belt a ballad, bust a rhyme, and break a move on the dance floor like nobody's business. See them on tour, find them in the record stores, listen for them on your favorite radio stations, or watch for their brand-new videos on TV.

The Backstreet Boys have quickly soared to the top. But they're just getting started. These five hunks plan to stay superstars and keep hitting the charts for a long time to come.

Think a good thing can't last forever? Not

according to Nick. He wants to assure all fans, "No matter what happens, if any of us go off, we're always going to be a group and we're always going to come back together. The Backstreet Boys' name will always be there, no matter what."

Keep the Backstreet Pride Alive!

# PART FOUR

# BSB FAST FACTS
# AND FUN STUFF

13. Fast Facts

# Kevin

Full name: Kevin Scott Richardson
Nickname: Train
Birthdate: October 3, 1972
Star sign: Libra
Birthplace: Lexington, KY
Favorite color: royal blue
Favorite television show: *Roseanne*
Favorite sounds: R. Kelly, Babyface, Prince,
    Teddy Riley
Hobbies: waterskiing, weightlifting, surfing,
    playing basketball and hockey

Favorite food: Asian

Instruments: keyboards, bass, vocals

Pets: a cat named Quincy

Relationship status: single

Image: mature and sophisticated

Fun fact: Kevin played Aladdin at Disney
World.

## *Howie*

Full name: Howard Dwaine Dorough

Nickname: Howie D, Sweet D

Birthdate: August 22, 1973

Star sign: Leo

Birthplace: Orlando, FL

Favorite color: purple

Favorite movie: *Willy Wonka and the Chocolate
Factory*

Favorite television shows: *Seinfeld, Married . . .
With Children*

Favorite sounds: Jon Secada, Bobby Brown

Hobbies: dancing, waterskiing, playing racquetball, working out

Favorite food: Asian
Instruments: guitar, vocals
Pets: none
Relationship status: single
Image: Latin lover
Fun fact: Howie irons his pajamas!

# Brian

Full name: Brian Thomas Littrell
Nickname: B-Rok
Birthdate: February 20, 1975
Star sign: Pisces
Birthplace: Lexington, KY
Favorite color: forest green
Favorite date movies: *Sleepless in Seattle, While
You Were Sleeping*
Favorite television show: *Fresh Prince of Bel-Air*
Favorite sounds: Boyz II Men, Bobby Brown
Hobbies: playing Nintendo or basketball with
Nick, weightlifting, listening to music
Favorite food: macaroni and cheese
Instruments: vocals

Pets: a cat named Missy
Relationship status: single
Image: funny guy
Fun fact: Brian sang gospel as a child.

# A.J.

Full name: Alexander James McLean
Nickname: Bone
Birthdate: January 9, 1978
Star sign: Capricorn
Birthplace: West Palm Beach, FL
Favorite color: purple
Favorite date movie: *Ghost*
Favorite television show: *Married . . . With Children*
Favorite sounds: Barrie McKnight
Hobbies: dancing, writing poetry, cartooning, shooting pool, playing volleyball
Favorite food: McDonald's burgers
Instruments: bass, vocals
Pets: a dachshund named Toby Wan Kenobi
Relationship status: single

Image: party boy
Fun fact: A.J. is a ventriloquist and puppeteer.

# *Nick*

Full name: Nickolas Gene Carter
Nickname: Nick
Birthdate: January 28, 1980
Star sign: Aquarius
Birthplace: Jamestown, NY
Favorite color: green
Favorite date movie: *I Love Trouble*
Favorite television shows: *The X-Files, The Simpsons, Mad About You*
Favorite sounds: Nirvana, Oasis, AC/DC, Prince, Jodeci
Hobbies: playing Nintendo and basketball with Brian, reading poetry, scuba diving
Favorite food: pizza
Instruments: drums, guitar, vocals
Pets: a terrier named Boo Boo and a cat named Pinky
Relationship status: single

Image: young, fresh-faced heartthrob
Fun fact: Nick's dad had to build a fence around
his home to keep Nick's fans at bay.

# 14. Boys Will Be Boys

## Kevin

*On the girl of his dreams:*

"I see her as sexy, or to be more exact, sensual. Without ignoring the qualities a girl has, her personality is very important to me, her energy, her presence, her appearance."

*On the sweetest thing a girl has done for him:*

"Probably the coolest thing was when I was really sick and this girl I was dating called her mother to get the recipe for chicken noodle soup and she made it for me from scratch."

*On music:*

"I'm really interested in all aspects of music. You know, I love what I do, but one day a time will come when I want to do something a little different, maybe working in the studio, producing or something."

*On being an old-fashioned boy:*

"My mom and dad taught me to be polite, so I always believe in opening the car door for a lady, pulling her chair out when she sits down, and letting her order food first."

*On asking girls out:*

"I'm sort of shy when it comes to making a first move. I like to become friends first so I can tell if they're going to be interested in me."

## Howie

*On appearances:*

"I'd still love a girl just as much if she wasn't gorgeous, because beauty is just skin deep and there are so many things like personality, humor, and goodness that can make someone beautiful on the inside. It's a mixture of all that that would succeed in seducing me."

*On the girl of his dreams:*

"The girl of my dreams would be my partner, in my personal life as well as in my career. I think it's important, no, essential, that we can build and live a life together."

*On showbiz:*

"You get a lot more rejection in the business than you do acceptance. You've got to keep on striving."

*On the BSB style:*

"We consider ourselves pop R&B. A lot of our style comes from the blues and gospel. Brian and A.J. grew up in gospel churches. Even though we lived in different areas, we all grew up listening to the same style of music."

*On writing songs:*

"Some of the ballads I've written have been about past experiences and I even sang them to the people concerned. When I was in high school,

I was walking along the beach with my date when I started singing the song I'd written for her. It's always very heartwarming when that happens."

*On communicating:*

"I prefer to talk from my heart and go with the way I feel."

# *Brian*

*On having a good sense of humor:*

"I think you've got to take life day by day, and the more humor you find in everyday things, then the happier you'll be. My grandmother on my dad's side is nearly eighty, but she looks like she's fifty and acts like she's thirty!"

*On best pal Nick:*

"One thing is for sure. If Nick wasn't in the group, it just wouldn't be the same for me."

*On fans:*

"Since we started, we've been really lucky with some of the people who support us—we've got some brilliant fans. There are loads who've stuck with us since the very beginning, and most of them we know real well. We literally sit on the plane going, 'Oh, do you think Helen or Louise or whoever will be at the airport?'"

*On having his heart broken:*
"I was two-timed by a girl in high school. I liked her and she liked someone else! I was disappointed, because she didn't turn out to be the girl I thought she was."

# A.J.

*On Christmas presents for the band:*
"For Kev, I want to get some rave clothes, and for Howie, one of the body shirts he wears. I'll probably get Nick a video game and B-Rok a pair of phat sunglasses."

*On piercings and tattoos:*
"I'd love to get my eyebrows pierced and to get three tattoos done. I'd have one on my back between my shoulder blades—a sun about as big

as three Coke cans. Then on my left arm, my nickname, 'Bone,' and on my right arm a Japanese word that means 'Eternal Life.'"

*On being linked with the Spice Girls:*
"Yeah, 'Howie or A.J. is involved with Melanie B . . .' or whoever. I wouldn't put it past any of the tabloids to say that so-and-so's with so-and-so. But it's cool, because that's when you start to know you are becoming someone."

*On a New Year's resolution:*
"I'm going to try to chill out on the McDonald's food. Sometimes I eat too much of it. I'm trying to eat less greasy, fattening foods and take better care of myself."

*On "mooning":*
"We've done it on the tour bus a couple of times when the guys on our band bus have pulled up next to us at the traffic lights. But we don't moon at anyone else. I don't want strangers taking pictures of my bum!"

# Nick

*On his dream girl:*

"There are some models that I think are fine. But what I want is somebody who has a good heart and a great personality."

*On his looks:*

"I think my ears are too big. They stick out too far."

*On girls liking him:*

"It's really flattering. I love the attention and I always think, 'Why do they like me?' Hopefully, they like my voice and my personality. I'd rather it wasn't just because of the way I look!"

*On his buddy Brian:*

"We really are so close. It's hard to say exactly why we get on so well . . . our personalities just seem to have clicked."

*On a serious relationship:*

"I don't have enough time to think about

starting a serious relationship with a girl I like. Hey, I'm only seventeen; I've got my whole life ahead of me to worry about that."

# 15. How Street-Smart Are You? A BSB Quiz

1. The BSB took their name from:
    a. the name of Howie's street
    b. a local club
    c. a market in downtown Orlando
    d. the name of the gym they go to
    e. a favorite restaurant

2. Which BSB has had his luggage lost most often while on the road?
    a. Kevin
    b. Howie
    c. A.J.
    d. Brian
    e. Nick

3. Which BSB likes Gummi Bears?
    a. Kevin
    b. Howie
    c. Nick
    d. Brian
    e. A.J.

4. Which hit single was the first one to go gold
   in Europe?
    a. "Quit Playin' Games"
    b. "I'll Never Break Your Heart"
    c. "We've Got It Goin' On"
    d. "Get Down"
    e. "If You Stay"

5. Which of the BSBs is nicknamed Train?
    a. Kevin
    b. Brian
    c. Howie
    d. A.J.
    e. Nick

6. Which BSB has a Southern accent?
    a. A.J.
    b. Brian

c. Howie

d. Kevin

e. Nick

7. Which BSB played Dopey in a grade school production of *Snow White and the Seven Dwarfs?*

    a. Howie

    b. Kevin

    c. A.J.

    d. Brian

    e. Nick

8. Nick recently cut his hair off because:

    a. He had dandruff

    b. Fans were pulling it out of his head

    c. He didn't like the way it looked

    d. He wanted to join the Army

    e. A fortuneteller told him to

9. Which is the song that was featured on the soundtrack of the motion picture *Booty Call*?

    a. "Get Down"

    b. "Boys Will Be Boys"

    c. "If You Stay"

d. "Anywhere for You"
e. "We've Got It Goin' On"

10. Which BSB is known to travel with his Playstation so he can play video games on the road?
a. Kevin
b. Nick
c. Brian
d. A.J.
e. Howie

# Answers

1. (c) The Boys took their name from a landmark market in downtown Orlando, Florida.

2. (b) Poor Howie has had his luggage lost most often!

3. (b) Howie is the Gummi Bar fanatic. Fans even toss them onstage!

4. (c) "We've Got It Goin' On" was the Boys' first number-one hit in Europe.

5. (a) The guys call Kevin "Train" because he tends to take charge.

6. (b) Kentucky-born Brian has an adorable Southern accent.

7. (c) A.J. played Dopey in grade school to wild acclaim!

8. (b) Believe it or not, Nick cut his hair so fans would stop pulling it.

9. (c) "If You Stay" was on the *Booty Call* soundtrack.

10. (b) Nick is the video game freak!

# 16. Where the Boys Are

Here's what the Boys are up to this summer: touring. Catch them if you can:

| | |
|---|---|
| 7/1–7/4/97 | Belgium |
| 7/5/97 | France |
| 7/6–7/11/97 | Promo-Dance Across USA/ICA Tour |
| 7/12/97 | San Antonio, TX |
| 7/13–7/17/97 | Promo-Dance Across USA/ICA Tour |
| 7/18/97 | Bentonville, AR—Wal-Mart Kickoff |
| 7/20–7/25/97 | U.S. dates to be announced |
| 7/26/97 | Cincinnati, OH |

| | |
|---|---|
| 7/27–7/30/97 | U.S. dates to be announced |
| 7/31–8/2/97 | Ibiza, Spain |
| 8/3–8/12/97 | Orlando |
| 8/13–8/17/97 | U.S. Promo/Wal-Mart |
| 8/18–9/4/97 | Germany |

17. *Discography*

# BACKSTREET BOYS
(European release)

**TRACKS:**
"We've Got It Goin' On"
"Anywhere for You"
"Get Down (You're the One for Me)"
"I'll Never Break Your Heart"
"Quit Playin' Games (With My Heart)"
"Boys Will Be Boys"
"Just to Be Close to You"
"I Wanna Be With You"
"Every Time I Close My Eyes"
"Darlin'"
"Let's Have a Party"

"Roll With It"
"Nobody But You"

# BACKSTREET BOYS

(American release)

**TRACKS:**

"We've Got It Goin' On"
"Quit Playin' Games (With My Heart)"
"Anywhere for You"
"If You Stay"
"I'll Never Break Your Heart"
"Get Down (You're the One for Me)"
"Set Adrift on Memory Bliss"
"If You Want It to Be Good, Girl (Get Yourself
    a Bad Boy)"
"Every Time I Close My Eyes"
"Boys Will Be Boys"
"Don't Leave Me"
"Tell Me That I'm Dreamin'"
"Tender Love"
"Just to Be Close to You"

# 18. The Ultimate BSB Dating Guide

**B**SB fans constantly dream about what it might be like to date their favorite Boy. Here's an idea of what a date with Kevin, Howie, Brian, A.J., or Nick could be!

## Kevin

Kevin is the most mature of the bunch. He might enjoy a cultural evening on the town. Don't forget—he likes girls who dress up, so get out your best outfit for this dream date. And remind Kevin to get his tux cleaned and pressed.

Kevin will call for his favorite girl with his

hands full of fragrant red roses. You remark how beautiful they are and set them in an elegant vase. There's not much time to waste. You're going to the ballet, and you've got a romantic box all to yourselves, stage left.

At the ballet, you both appreciate the beauty and grace of the dancers, and the muted tones of the accompanying orchestra. You're dazzled by the entire production of *Swan Lake, Coppelia, Sleeping Beauty*—whichever you have chosen. Kevin is engaged in the ballet, but not too engaged to keep his thoughts away from you.

After the ballet, it's a late dinner for you and Mr. Sophisticated. You remember that he enjoys Asian food, so the next stop is for sushi. When you arrive at the upscale Japanese restaurant, you are escorted to a private room. You and Kevin slip off your shoes and sit at a low table to share your delicacies from the Far East. Underneath the table, you are, of course, playing footsie.

The meal is delightful. But the night has

just begun. Don't forget that Kevin is an expert ballroom dancer. It's time to put on your dancing shoes.

The two of you dance the night away. Kevin's moves are so smooth, you feel like Cinderella at the ball. This handsome prince has definitely swept you off your feet!

It's late, and time to be heading home. Kevin drops you off, tells you what a wonderful time he's had. Then he plants a soft kiss right on your lips before he turns to go.

Sigh. It's been the best night of your life. You'll be seeing Kevin again in your dreams!

## Howie

They don't call Howie Mr. Romance for nothing. You are sure to have the time of your life with this Latin lover.

Howie enjoys the beach, so your date might start there. You pick out your best bikini for the day of sun and fun.

Howie comes to pick you up in his convertible. The sun is shining and there's not a cloud in the sky. You bound into his car and you're off to sample the surf.

At the beach, Howie takes your hand and leads you past the crowd. You walk over some rocks, and voilà—just past them is a secluded sandy spot. It's completely empty and the rocks block the view of the frolicking families and tourists on the other side. Alone at last.

You spread out your blanket and get ready to cozy up to your Backstreet babe. Howie has been carrying a huge picnic basket and you've been dying to know what's inside.

He tells you to close your eyes. When you open them again, you can't believe what you see.

Howie has spread out an elegant picnic lunch for two, including sparkling cider and strawberries in champagne flutes. Two silver candlesticks hold flickering candles, which is an adorable touch, since it is the middle of the day!

He tells you he's made the chicken and pasta salad himself, which is absolutely delicious. You've got quite a chef on your hands!

You're full, so the two of you lazily bake in

the sun for a while. Oops! Howie reminds you that you forgot to put on sunscreen. He gently rubs it into your back.

You take a dip later on, and Howie teases you with a splash fight. You're having so much fun that you barely notice it's getting dark. It's time to go home.

When Howie drops you off, he reaches into the picnic basket and tells you that he forgot dessert. He pulls out a pink frosted cupcake with a heart in the middle. Inside the heart is your name.

Your own heart melts. You give him a kiss and thank him for the best date you've ever had.

## *Brian*

You know you are in for a night of fun, fun, fun with Brian. He wants to surprise you, so he hasn't told you what you're doing yet.

When he arrives, he steps into your house and reaches into his jacket pocket. He pulls out a little package wrapped in gold. "For you," he says. It's a box of your favorite chocolates!

He says you don't have much time, so you hurry out to his car. On the dashboard are two tickets. You pick them up.

You can't believe it! You're going to see Jerry Seinfeld! He's your favorite comedian, and he's performing at the local arts center—but tickets have been sold out for months.

"Front row center," Brian tells you. "But we have dinner plans first."

Brian takes you to your favorite restaurant. It's a casual Southern-themed place. You love the fried chicken. Brian is happy because they serve their own homemade macaroni and cheese.

At dinner Brian makes you laugh. That's what you adore about him. He mimics the waiter, tells you a few jokes, makes some funny faces. You're in stitches the whole time.

After dinner it's off to the arts center. You are so close to Jerry Seinfeld you can almost reach out and touch him. His routines have you both laughing hysterically.

Then Jerry starts asking the audience questions. He comes to Brian. "Where are you from and who are you with?" Jerry asks him.

Brian stands up. "I'm Brian Littrell, I'm from Lexington, Kentucky, and I'm with the most beautiful girl in the world," he tells the entire crowd.

You glow with pride. This is definitely the most amazing date you've ever had.

## A.J.

You have no idea what A.J. McLean has up his sleeve for tonight. But he did tell you that he wanted to take you out for your birthday.

He told you to dress funky. So you've got on the coolest clothes in your closet.

When A.J. gets to your house, he pulls out a blindfold. "I don't want you to know where you're going until the very last minute," he explains.

You put on the blindfold and he leads you out to his car. He steals a kiss from you before he opens the door.

You drive for a while, and your mind is spinning with the possibilities. You feel the car come to a stop. A.J. helps you out of the car.

"Can I take the blindfold off yet?" you ask. A.J. says no and asks you not to peek.

He leads you, slowly, into a building. It's very quiet. Right before he unties the blindfold, he whispers into your ear, "Happy Birthday, baby."

The blindfold comes off. "Surprise!" voices shout.

You blink slowly. You are in a huge club. It's the first time you've ever been in one. There, standing before you, is your family and all of your friends. A.J. even flew in your best friend, who moved away last year, for the occasion.

You can't believe that he's organized a surprise party just for you. You throw your arms around A.J. and thank him.

"Come with me," he says, and leads you to the stage.

You stop dead in your tracks. You can't believe what you see. Standing there are the other four Backstreet Boys. A.J. introduces you to the gang, then they break out into a birthday song for you.

A.J. holds your hand and serenades you as the boys croon behind him. You feel like you are the queen of the universe.

Next, a d.j. puts on some slammin' dance tunes, and you and A.J. dance the night away with your family and friends.

You knew A.J. was a party boy. And he made sure *you* had a birthday party you would never forget.

## *Nick*

Nick picks you up in a limo for your date. You're excited—you've never been in one before. This one has a sun roof, a television set, a VCR, and enough snacks and sodas for an army. "Where are we going?" you ask Nick.

"Anywhere you want," he responds.

Nick has rented the limo for the whole night. He wants you to call the shots. You can go anywhere, do anything.

You and Nick first started liking each other when you beat him at Mortal Kombat. So your first stop, you decide, is the video arcade.

You play for an hour or two, laughing and holding hands. Nick wins some games, you win others. You're having a great time.

You're hungry, so it's back to the limo. You tell the driver to take you to Rock 'n' Roll Pizza, your favorite eatery. There, you get a large pepperoni pie, and listen to a cover band that's playing tunes by all the groups you love.

Nick takes your hand when you're finished and you join the crowd on the dance floor.

Whew! You're exhausted after what seems like the millionth dance, but the band is so good, you couldn't stop. You slide back into your booth and Nick asks you where you'd like to go next.

You suggest a late movie, and the limo whisks you over to the local movie theater. Perfect! The new action flick you've been dying to see is playing. Nick is psyched, too.

In the theater, you share a tub of popcorn and cuddle up to your dreamy date during some of the suspenseful scenes. What a night it has been!

# 19. Throw Your Own BSB Party

**Y**ou can throw a party with all your friends who adore the guys just as much as you do. All you need is your Backstreet Boys CD and some paper and pens.

To kick off the party, play "Let's Have a Party" at top volume. Sing along with party boy A.J. when he says "All I wanna know is where the party's at!"

Then take out the pens and paper. Each girl has to write a love letter to her favorite BSB. As you work, of course, make sure there are BSB tunes in the background.

When you're done writing, take turns reading the letters out loud. Then vote for the one you think is the best.

Of course, your BSB party should have plenty of snacks. After the love letter competition, it's time to pig out. If you have a BSB video, pop it in and study the Boys' moves while you eat.

For the next game, divide into small groups. Pick out your favorite BSB tune and make up a dance routine to go along with it. Everyone gets a chance to perform and vote.

To top things off, you might want to design your *own* ultimate BSB dream dates.

Remember those love letters you wrote? Mail them to the Boys! Tell them you're planning another BSB party and let them know when it might be. You never know who might call the next time. . . .

# 20. What the Stars Say

**W**ith the U.S. release of their album, the year ahead promises to be an exciting one for the Boys. Here's what's in the stars for each BSB:

### Kevin—LIBRA

Overall, it seems that Libras may have an energetic year ahead. Kevin may need to be cautious, however, not to overdo it, and to allow himself plenty of downtime in his schedule. By the end of the year, Kevin may find that he is taken very seriously as a singer and a musician. This may mean other prospects for him. Don't worry, though. There's no sign of his leaving the band. There's a chance Kevin may use his keyboard skills in a different capacity, like playing on an album for another band. People close to Kevin could notice him taking a new approach to the band and his personal life.

## LOVE/SOCIAL LIFE

Libras are headed for an active love and social life over the next year, and Kevin will most likely be as popular as ever. He can probably expect a lot of invites while the planets influence his fifth house of parties and romance, especially around the new year.

## HOME/FAMILY

There's a possibility Kevin could feel overwhelmed in this area. Perhaps with his busy social schedule his family may be feeling neglected. Not to worry, though; as a Libra, Kevin is sure to strike the right balance between career and family. After the new year, it looks like things will ease up for him and he will be able to spend quality time with his mom and siblings.

## HEALTH

Libras won't have any major health concerns, as long as they eat right and try to avoid stress. Kevin is conscientious about working out, so he is sure to be in tip-top shape for the year to come. Plus, there is a lot of energy for Libras in the year ahead, so Kevin is bound to take advantage of that. The spring looks to be invigorating for him—he just may get in a lot of waterskiing during that time.

## CAREER

Libras' year ahead shows a highly creative time for Kevin. Signs point to the fact that he may be putting a lot of his energy into songwriting and other ambitious projects. The holiday season doesn't seem to be as productive as the other months. It may be a good time for Kevin to catch up with his family and take a vacation.

## *Howie*—LEO/VIRGO

In general, those on the cusp of Leo and Virgo can look forward to good luck with relationships and finances. There's the distinct possibility that

Howie may have the Midas touch in invest-
ments. All of Howie's relationship areas look
good: family, friends, and, most especially,
romance.

## LOVE/SOCIAL LIFE

It looks like Howie may be a good corre-
spondent over the next year. Leos will be making
a lot of phone calls, and writing a lot of letters.
Hopefully Howie will keep up with his fan mail!
Howie never likes to miss out on any social occasion, but he may find it hard to tear himself
away from work during the holiday season.
Because it is a good year for Leo and Virgo relationships, this might be the time when Howie
meets Ms. Right.

## HOME/FAMILY

September may be a good time for Howie
to make changes in his domestic life. He might
purchase a house as a permanent home base off
the road. Whatever changes he might make in
his living situation, the stars show that he will
probably stick close to his family.

## HEALTH

Leos will be active for the greater part of the next year. They may have to watch their diet, however, and not overdo it during the holiday season. Virgos should be cautioned that too much work may result in exhaustion. It may be important for Howie to take time off when the BSB tour wraps up.

## CAREER

Virgo forecasts a busy year ahead with lots of rewards. Howie could be exploring new territory in his career as well.. He just might bring his newly learned guitar skills to the stage in the fall or winter. In spring and summer, Leos will make a lot of leaps. Howie possibly may move further into guitar virtuosity. Again, he has to be cautious about overworking, especially during the holiday season.

## *Brian*—PISCES/AQUARIUS

The year ahead promises both discipline and extravagance for those born under the Pisces sign. Aquarius' can count on many exciting changes and may begin to acquire valuable possessions this year. Since Brian is on the cusp of both of these signs, he may even do something wild such as starting to collect rock 'n' roll memorabilia from his musical idols, Boyz II Men and Bobby Brown. Brian may also spend a lot of money over the holiday season on generous gifts for the band and family and friends, though he may worry about it later. But it will all work out in the end, and Brian may feel silly for having fretted so much. He may spend a great deal of time on his vocal and dance skills, working long, hard, disciplined hours. By the spring and summer, Brian may want to spend time alone to recharge.

## LOVE/SOCIAL LIFE

Early in the fall, the stars show, Brian may become more involved in charity or volunteer work. He's a good communicator, so it may be an area that has to do with social skills or counseling. This could take up a lot of his social time, but he will probably feel fulfilled with the project of his choice. In his love life, Brian may unfortunately see little action. He will be way too busy with other pursuits.

## HOME/FAMILY

Leos may feel a need for nurturing around November. It would be the prime time for Brian to visit his home in Kentucky. During that time he may be thinking a lot about his childhood and rekindling past relationships with old friends.

## HEALTH

Brian might feel some anxiety about his finances. But it will all be for nothing. He may begin a regimented diet and exercise program that will keep stress at bay. But signs point to Brian sticking with his program and seeing incredible results by the summer.

## CAREER

It is likely that Brian will have support and encouragement from his bandmates, making it a breezy year on tour for him. He just may be at his vocal best, and will probably put a lot of effort into his stage presence.

## *A.J.*——CAPRICORN

Capricorns have a carefree year ahead of them. There's a chance A.J. will get a fabulous lucky break in the fall, perhaps involving his finances. He may make a very wise and fruitful investment.

### LOVE/SOCIAL LIFE

Party boy A.J. could be in rare form in the next year. There's a chance he will be busy bonding with old friends and making many new friends. There might be many nights of dancing till dawn, especially around the holiday season. But A.J.'s youth will probably work for him—he won't tire easily. His planets may be in line for him to impress a special someone in the late fall, if he seizes the opportunity rather than letting it pass.

### HOME/FAMILY

Capricorns will have to make sure their personal lives are in order this year. A.J.'s carefree attitude may make him neglect some private matters. The stars indicate he may be closer than ever to family members, especially in the spring and summer.

## HEALTH

A.J. will probably not have any health problems, despite his love for staying out late. He will most likely stay in good shape, but he may have to go easy on the fatty foods to keep his energy at the level he needs. A.J. may have to "just say no" to fast food a few times!

## CAREER

There's a chance A.J. may be looking to improve himself in many areas, especially his career. The stars show that he may be interested in taking a class that is career related, but doesn't necessarily focus on performance. He may end up studying music management or even delving into rock 'n' roll history!

## *Nick*—AQUARIUS

The next year will be full of growth and significant and beneficial changes for Aquarians. The stars show that it is a good time for Nick to experiment with his look, and to broaden his social circle.

## LOVE/SOCIAL LIFE

Nick may be very active socially. He could be dating a lot, and not just one girl. Dating could bring him new friends, and he would be getting out more. He may have to watch out, though, for some new acquaintances who may spread gossip with the intention of hurting someone's feelings.

## HOME/FAMILY

It is likely that Nick will be doing a lot of physical and personal growth over the next year. Sometimes he may not understand the changes he is going through. The stars show Nick bonding with family members, which could prove to be comforting for him. Nick may be calling home for advice frequently when he is on the road.

## HEALTH

Aquarians need to be realistic about their abilities and not go to extremes when working out or playing sports. Nick may have a lot of stamina, but should keep it in check to avoid injury in sports such as basketball or football. He also should be careful weightlifting and not take on more than he can handle. Nick's diet will most likely be healthier than ever, though. Perhaps he will pass up that slice of pizza for some healthy pasta instead.

## CAREER

Nick is going to win even more fans with the debut of the BSB album in the U.S. He is sure to be in the public eye more than usual throughout the year. His popularity will be at an all-time high. Nick's father might have to build an even higher fence!

The astrological year ahead will be busy and productive for all the Backstreet babes. It will be interesting to see whether the Boys follow the paths the stars predict!

## 21. Which Backstreet Boy Is Your Best Love Match?

**Y**ou may think you know which Backstreet Boy is the perfect guy for you—but what do the stars have to say about it? All you need to know is your birthdate, and you can figure out which Backstreet Boy you would make beautiful music with!

If your birthday is from:

March 21 to April 19, you are an ARIES. Howie and Brian are your best love matches.
April 20 to May 20, you are a TAURUS. A.J. and Brian are your best love matches.

May 21 to June 20, you are a GEMINI. Kevin
and Howie are your best love matches.

June 21 to July 22, you are a CANCER. Howie
and Brian are your best love matches.

July 23 to August 22, you are a LEO. Kevin is
your best love match.

August 23 to September 22, you are a VIRGO.
A.J. is your best love match.

September 23 to October 21, you are a LIBRA.
Kevin and Nick are your best love matches.

October 22 to November 21, you are a
SCORPIO. Brian, A.J., and Howie are
your best love matches.

November 22 to December 21, you are a
SAGITTARIUS. Howie and Nick are
your best love matches.

December 22 to January 19, you are a CAPRI-
CORN. Brian is your best love match.

January 20 to February 18, you are an AQUAR-
IUS. Nick is your best love match.

February 19 to March 20, you are a PISCES.
Nick is your best love match.

*Want to get in on the BSB excitement? You can join their official fan club by writing to:*

> **Backstreet Boys Fan Club**
> **P.O. Box 618225**
> **Orlando, FL 32861**

For a fee, new members receive a membership card, a group photo, a BSB button, a BSB pen, a quarterly newsletter, and a 10 percent discount on BSB merchandise.

But wait, there's more! The best part is that fan club members get preferred advance seating for concerts and could win a chance to meet the Boys.

You can also visit the BSB official website at www.backstreetboys.com, or call their hotline at 407-880-7000. Please note this is a toll call!

# About the Author

K. S. Rodriguez is an avid music and movie fan. She worked many years as a book editor and is also the author of *Jackie Chan: The Most Dangerous Hands in Hollywood*, also published by HarperActive. Ms. Rodriguez lives in New York City with her husband, Ronnie.